a berserker stuck in traffic

by erik richardson

Pebblebrook Press

an imprint of *Stoneboat*—www.stoneboatwi.com.

"We can keep from a child all knowledge of earlier myths, but we cannot take from him the need for mythology."

—*Carl Gustav Jung*

acknowledgments

My grateful acknowledgment to the editors of the following journals in which these poems first appeared.

Arbor Vitae: "borrowed light," "suburbaphobia," "constellations of fate"

Centrifugal Eye: "permuted merton"

Chiron Review: "on the dangers of reading the bhagavad gita during my lunch break at the office," "heaney whispers"

Free Verse: "time and tide"

Nerve Cowboy: "a berserker stuck in traffic"

Stoneboat: "hemingway's alchemy," "if god were an impressionist"

Three Cup Morning: "earth in the future imperfect tense"

Verse Wisconsin: "on the edge of heatstroke," "ouranos falls in love"

Special thanks to B.J. Best, Cathryn Cofell, and Michael Kriesel.

a berserker stuck in traffic ©2014 by Pebblebrook Press, an imprint of *Stoneboat*. Editors: Lisa Vihos, Rob Pockat, Signe Jorgenson, Jim Giese. Cover photo: Dan Kinsey, binz187@yahoo.com ©2014. ISBN: 978-0692251324

⟶ Indicates no stanza break

For Tess

contents

if god were an impressionist

if an impressionist had designed the world
there would be no edges sharp enough to cut
and letters and books would be far too blurry to read.

water would be made of blue and white cobblestones,
of course. our hair would look like bird nests
as the fun-house mirrors would never show true.

there would be no rainforests or deserts
only lilypad ponds, and manicured parks,
and fields of poppies or wheat spreading to the edges.

everyone would live near the bumpy water,
like the sea coast and the river's edge,
riddled with sailboats or steamships or both.

and what night sky fireworks there would be
with every planet and orange-white-hurricane star
twisting and twirling the dark around it

while all along the street, smudged ballerinas
would sit in sidewalk cafés with gray-bearded men
with umbrellas and top hats, murmuring in french.

erik richardson

ouranos falls in love

so what if her waist-to-hip ratio is not the right number?
her inner balance outweighs her outer asymmetry
her heart is iron strong
and she is filled with passionate fire
her mass attracts me, gives me weight
her geography is majestic
and no map can capture all she really is

suburbaphobia

perched on the edge of 92nd street
stressed for infecting my neighbors' yards
with wind transmitted diseases—

incriminating dandelions point back to me
even in the dark—I have no clear idea
what time the sun died today or will rise again.

denial is my only refuge.
if I should accidentally look up into the sky,
I will float free of my moorings

past oak tops and clouds
with electric moon-glow edges
into the thinner air, thinking of light things

like dandelion whiskers,
mylar birthday balloons,
and the first time I saw my daughter

play in the snow.

erik richardson

cancer ride at disney world

once upon warm eyefuls of sun
palm trees led us to our sensible white rental ford
watched tall afternoons at the pool
and stood like signposts all the while
we followed that florida highway sun-poached
looking for a beach

once reflected in lazy colors
palm trees shaded by their own green dreads
tried to warn us, too late
to knock the apple from snow white's hand,
we wound our way through the waiting lines
to steel-drum sounds of clanking rides

now I stare into mid-winter skies
palm trees can't survive this northern life
my fingertips here on the pale window sting
like the sharp-edged shards from mirror, mirror
raised in held-breath silence
to save us if frost should fail

the book of kells

o, you glorious woman
glowing with age
how long since you have been read
out loud by anyone who knows
the old tongue hiding under the latin
on your tattooed, vellum skin unkissed,
shrouded in a veil

of christianity? they no longer wonder
at how you stray from the other gospels.
your ancient symbols breathe softly—
with every unspoken word between the lines
the monks grew dizzy, too flail drunk
to find the truth twisted
among the beautiful curves

of your body language. what is there
is just too easy. a lover would know
better than to merely hear
the things you seem to say.
with iron door handles and hinges
binding you fast, too long
with the celibate,

shaved heads who believed
you were only as deep as them,
shutting you up, indoors,
far from sounds of passion
reeling fiddles, singing,
drum beats, waves on the shore,
rain on fields

whispering against your spine.
gather the old symbols around you
like swarming ravens colored
with black gall ink. let it cost them,
loveless men, dearly to try to hold you
in silence. come away with me.
be spoken.

erik richardson

the river shannon

eating the salmon from connla's well,
in the fabled hall of the fairy king
gave wisdom, so the old stories say—

myths that mothered the dream of yeats
where the fish fed on crimson berries
falling from nine circling hazel trees

sionna broke the men-only rule
and gave her life to the flooding well
birthing the river that nourished the land

from underground streams on cuilcagh mountain
all the way to her grandfather's sea
what wisdom, then, was gained?

none from the hazelnuts,
none from the salmon.
just an irish woman's heart:

let go of everything else
and climb down into the well
that's how to become immortal, a river—

no clinging, no standing still,
needing no map but your own sacrifice
as gravity pulls you down

let your fertile spirit be swallowed alike
by hot-blooded warriors and dusty monks
with ink-stained fingers and tongues

love all your children the same,
and shelter them from invaders when you can
hide their bones beneath your tears when you can't

birr castle, county offaly

shadows shift and move across
cold gray stones drifting in wind and clouds
an ancient castle cuts through rolling waves
of earth, pennants flying.
someone's on board besides the ghosts
of nine generations past
since these queen-blessed pirates sailed
over land, stone keel crushing our native tongue,
so much that was our own
and free. these land-locked aristocrats,
living and dead, are sinking slowly down.
peat leaking into the rock-ribbed hull
pulls them under the surface of earth and moat at last,
plundering days long gone,
buried treasure spent,
ship's cannons rusted over by the stubborn irish rain.

erik richardson

missouri morning

at 65 mph my gurney cuts the early morning
fog that lies heavy between rumpled hills
in fall along the muddy missouri
while the river moves slow and steady
like oxycontin, dulling memories,
barging through the current
of my veins.
it's been a year since mom died.
I finally brought myself home
to pick up the family photo albums.
even memories of her are sharp.
turning pages of a past life
cut the lines where fresh stitches railroad
across the palms of my hands.
the radio fades in and out
as my electric green blip traces a path
up and down
the rolling line of hills
one hand sucking in heat
from the styrofoam cup of coffee, breakfast.
I think about how she couldn't speak
a simple kindness or stand silent. ever
her mouth was filled with jagged glass
that sliced us when she spoke.
I listen to the low hum—
steel-belted radials on the road—
and try to ignore the friction of the seatbelt
against the track spur of stitches just above my heart,
where I jammed the letter opener
to let in light.

→

with the smell of damp morning woods
whipping in through the window,
the cool oxygen lights up behind my eyes
and I see she could never forgive herself.
the doctor's voice cutting in
on my radio, whenever I top a hill,
tells me I'm better off since I stopped
and sent the albums arcing from the bridge
to be swallowed by the muddy mo.

on the dangers of reading the bhagavad gita during my lunch break at the office

standing on his great office chair
yoked with white computer cords
he sounds his great conch
and tumult echoes through heaven and earth.

the lesser versions of you
are trapped in a plastic cage
of your own stubborn making.
what use to us, o computer,
are promotions, delights, or life itself?

spin an odd number of times
else it won't come true.
go clockwise against the earth
and centrifugal force
will throw the world away from you
for a second so you can
breathe. before it closes in
again, decide to be someone
new—your own opposite,
an immortal eastern prince,
as a man discards worn out clothes.

when his computer had spoken
he halted the splendid aeron chair
between the arrayed cubicles
of competing departments

never have I not existed,
nor you, nor these filing cabinets,
and never in the future
shall we cease to exist.

he is set apart by his disinterest
toward comrades, clients, enemies,
foes, friends, mid-level managers,
good and evil secretaries.

your house will look different
when you go home, it will be
haunted with clutter
from some dull stranger
from a previous life.

quickly collect the shiny shards
of the cracked plastic
put them in a bag on the curb,
and let the old tenant be carried away.

when one is free of individuality
and his understanding is untainted,
even if he quits this job,
he does not quit and is not bound.

heaney whispers

sitting in the dublin airport where runways left
a surgical scar in the midst of green-bellied fields
the country stares at me through heaney's eyes
through time. his picture whispers from the terminal wall
of railway children and telegraph wires
slightly out of place here. the whispers
move on through, me waiting like others before for a plane
with scalpel wings to sever me, history.
as the wings slice, peat-black shadows
bleed out to pool under me under crumbled ruins
unhealed and held in place
by rain and dark, by vigilant sheep, tangled
with winding roads
themselves cut through time
through the midst of green-bellied fields.

kung fu theater

sprawled on the speckled old carpet
in the family room summer
saturday afternoons,
dad half-dozing in the recliner,
we watched old kansas city channel 41
to see what new style or secret technique
would be unleashed that week.

every white-haired old man in the village
a candidate to be the legendary master
all-but-forgotten, waiting in secret,
for a student with a noble cause.
would it be the gardener? the drunk?
the blind cook at the noodle house?
no master ever appeared to teach me

to throw the deadly dragon fist of shaolin
or meet swords and arrows with iron skin
to save the village from a horde of villains
or even my family, years later, from dad.
part of me long since moved on, slowly
becoming one of the old men
in a story of my own, no master

but better each year. perhaps I will be
ready. be able to move my lips in chinese
but speak in english,
when some young person turns to me
to help him save his village from an evil army,
maybe just his sister.
a part of me is still ten, glued to the tube,

slouched against the base of the couch,
soaking it in, warm summer sun
oozing through the back screen door,
watching to see who it turns out to be this time,
who will break out the dusty manual
of the shadowless kick, or the tiger's claw—
maybe the white-haired, old school teacher.

absolute values

there we stood in church, wrapped in nothing
but our absolute values. with church lights
forming the stiff, straight bracket lines
binding us in place in mexico, missouri.
as you clenched my hand

as hard as january ice. you cried.
I could think of nothing else
so I leaned over and kissed you
ahead of schedule. and yet too late
or too soon, both the same distance

like our wandering gypsy years since—
back and forth between positive and negative.
but when you laugh in the early morning light
all plus and minus signs covering us fall away
and I start over at zero.

earth in the future imperfect tense

with emery richardson, age 6

a circle is a line that never stops
since it never turns any corners
like the shape of the moon
or its path through the dark
or an equator edge on the head of a pin
where medieval angels would gather to dance
in infinite numbers in a circular waltz

since it never turns any corners
it can't cross over itself
this truth fails if the circle is tilted,
unbalanced by a wobble of guilt
and the fear it can never be pure again
even if washed in a crystal blue sea
and bleached by a circular sun

it can't cross over itself
so it must keep on going to infinity
weighted down by gravity tossed
or tripping on the cluttered remnants of youth
or stumbling from the spin and the tilt
the dancers fail and start to unwind
like a nautilus shell from that salty sea
turning into the future incomplete

permuted merton

Because the heavenly stars
Stand in a ring:
And all the pieces of the mosaic, earth,
Get up and fly away like birds.
—Thomas Merton

get up and fly away
condescending monk
because the mosaic birds
and all the pieces of the earth,
stand in a ring
like heavenly stars

stand in a ring
like pieces of the mosaic earth
your god should not have let you hide
because the heavenly stars
and all the birds
get up and fly away

stand up like birds
be a father to your illegitimate child
and get all of the heavenly stars
in a ring because the pieces
and the mosaic earth
fly away

and the heavenly pieces
of the earth get up and fly away
like mosaic birds
because the stars
all stand in a ring
as silent as the penance you still owe

borrowed light

the farmer in the photograph
rides on a solitary summer day
forever, in august maybe
on the rolling missouri plain

tractor tracks in field grass
mark the mower's circuit of days
sympathetic shadow lines
carved in the silvery green

glowing under black-winged clouds
like ravens
a late summer rain coming in
carried by a rusted red tractor

across the shifting slopes
the past is dragged forward
in a low, pa-dumping gear
coughing and lurching

toward the barn against the wind
eye blinks, shutter clicks
black feathers fossilize
suspended waiting for gravity's call

but with the next breath rocks will turn
again to smoke, and rain
will gradually bleed the colors away
for the fall

into grace and winter
staring at a farmer now
in his dusty hall a part of me
will stay behind, like stone

in summer missouri fields

erik richardson

on the edge of heatstroke

I remember the hot august texas sun
setting fire to the edges of an earlier life
drill sergeant shouting strings
of commands to march us about
like militant marionettes
in step after endless step
some days warning flags rose like mercury
their message clear:
do not expect recruits to march today.

I remember your anger cooking my skin
last night like too many others
age and change have worn me down
since that texas summer
since last night
this is not enough, it's too much
like something by tennessee williams
I am still untrained and untrainable.
your temper is pushing me to heatstroke,
so I plunge my head in a glass of beer
to cool my tongue-scorched brain.

my life is burning away in my hands
as I tell you this
the lengthening ash falls onto the table
if only the fire would jump and spread
to my strings and let me down
and let me drown the heat and smoke
in spilled cold beer. warning flags rise:
if you pull my strings,
I'll walk.

time and tide

4-yr-old daughter splashing tub
every corner and bend of her hiding sand
the number of grains measuring the day
building tide pools in the middle of summer
on the windy lake michigan shore

waves pushing in walls crumbling
erosion speeding like a time-lapsed film
a girl and two parents moving faster
counterclockwise keeping the pools intact
let the rising water in but slowly

later now playfully sloshing
our own little tub standing in for a lake
fingers and toes wriggling raisined
fleeting illusions of premature age

water draining leaving lines of sand
tracing out the flow of tide and time
like a spilled hourglass

erik richardson

hemingway's alchemy

breathing deep I wait for the secret shapes of words
to appear. in that blank-page moment,
he and I are almost one.
until my stumbling, clumsy fingers begin to type,
unable to follow where the symbols would lead.
each clack a failed deciphering step
on a staircase of mystical keys.
our elements all the same—consonant, vowel, comma,
in undissolved mixture with empty spaces.
for me the keys will never turn to gold,
but I've learned his final lesson well—
that bottle always close at hand
has a trigger at the end,
fires tiny drops of lead
that will not transmute.

classroom astronomy

stepping through the doorway
of my classroom, like other teachers,
I am squeezed and stretched
through a wormhole,
hurtling me out among the stars,
to look around in weightless wonder
at the sky full of 3rd-graders.
it is hard for the other kids and me
to see you clearly— faint, beautiful child
like the blurry patch of the pleiades.
so many thoughts
you can't express—your light
passes through our telescopes too small
so your brilliance seems to shrink
still light years out.
maybe we shrink too. your emotions,
frustrations like hydrogen and helium
wrap you daily in dusty nebulae
clouding our sight.
what do you think about
god? infinity? even if you don't know
their names. are you happy?
would you have children—
birthing white dwarves or red giants
of your own—
if you knew they would be like you?
do you know how much you are
like a spectacle of stars?

erik richardson

fermat's last theorem

Equations of the form $x^n + y^n = z^n$ can have no non-zero solutions for any n greater than 2. "I have a truly marvelous demonstration of this proposition which this margin is too small to contain."

Pierre de Fermat in the margin of *Arithmetica*

once more I try to leap the theorem in a single bound
while fermat's exponents speckle my x-ray sight
the pen^3 + the paper^3 can never equal the cube of my thoughts
but at the level of squares they can.

here where pythagoras sits forever trapped
in two dimensions like a villain from that superman movie
I spill my thoughts on paper, creating
an algebraic blur, but the solution is shielded in lead.

when I finally manage to clear my head, I swear
just like before, not to weaken again
so soaked in guinness, my yeasty kryptonite,
but time is a movement in four dimensions

and there the final theorem roams free.
even under a yellow sun my memory^4 + the stout's dark call^4
can never equal my good intentions times themselves
then times themselves, and yet again for the very fourth time.

a berserker stuck in traffic

or at a desk, staring at a screen.
standing in a long, slow line at the store,
when a valkyrie whispers in your ear,
"you were not born for this."
you remember that your bearskin shirt
is stashed in the bottom of your dresser,
but the trance is on. there is no drug like strength

like stepping out of your own skin
onto the prow of a ship in the cold north sea
the sound of creaking oars in your ears,
salt spray stinging your tongue
or a field where hammers sound on shields,
and skulls of those not in harmony with the whole
are left behind to feed the war-gulls.

then the light goes green. the line moves on.
your morning meds kick in
pulling you down like dwarf-forged chains, the rage
that would once have made you holy, battle-favored
of the hanged god, fading. pretend: you are just an accountant.
poems of the skalds were not true. a sword in the trunk
of your car is a really. bad. idea.

erik richardson

the turing tragedy

begin program :/
if brilliant, change figure
mathematician
proceed to [state: <college>]
hourglass
hourglass
a cambridge man
breaking crazy-assed german codes

anything that can be put into an algorithm
can be solved by a turing machine
the halting problem:
whether a man will stop running
when processing the feeling of loneliness

if the war ends, change figure
propose to a woman
proceed to [state: <spy farm>]
hourglass
hourglass
bletchley park
he chained his mug to the radiator pipes
to prevent being stolen

marriage won't fit into an algorithm
so he couldn't solve it, couldn't go through
computable, but he couldn't easily compute that it was

if your gay lover tries to rob you,
change figure,
go to [state: <court>]
hourglass
hourglass
female hormones, chemical castration
erase [subroutine: < prison term>]
insert [recursive loop: <depression>]

suicide by cyanide
like his favorite scene from snow white
who could blame him?

:/ end program

constellations of fate

I know I will never grow old
as I lie with the frozen earth
cradled in the curve
of my frost-prickled back

spiderweb strands of light
stretch from star to star to me
tracing in dark patience
silent shapes in the sleeping sky

old blind sisters, in groups of three,
suspended, spinning ethereal
threads of wyrd to measure our days
as they carousel around us

the cloud of my sword-lunged breath
freezes and falls away toward the light
of ancient days where giants stepped
from longboats into the unknown.

Erik Richardson lives in Milwaukee, Wisconsin, with his family and assorted pets. In addition to teaching, he attends grad school in psychology, coaches several award-winning robotics teams, and runs a small communications firm. He is a three-time winner

of the Gahagan Prize at the world's largest Irish festival, received honorable mention for the Hixson Award, and is a regular contributor to *Centrifugal Eye*. His work has appeared in *Nerve Cowboy, Verse Wisconsin,* and *Chiron Review* among others.

www.ingramcontent.com/pod-product-compliance
Lightning Source LLC
Chambersburg PA
CBHW051706040426
42446CB00009B/1325
* 9 7 8 0 6 9 2 2 5 1 3 2 4 *